Water

Thousands have lived without love, not one without water.

W.H. Auden

For my parents, who made water a big part of my life.

Contents

Author's Note

I have other projects I thought would be done by now. I began writing *Water* when I accepted that those projects were still coming, but later than I had hoped. *Water* came about because I felt stuck in other work. Writing this collection served me as a writer in a similar way as visiting the water has always served my spirit as a person. This process was a relief, a reprieve. It lengthened my patience and renewed my outlook, and so by taking a break from my other work to write *Water*, I was able to experience art mimicking life. Writing poetry *became* sitting by the water.

Vincent Moyet

Summer's End 2024

Part One

Musings

In time and with water, everything changes.

Leonardo da Vinci

1   **Water**

Drink from me and come to life,

be calm in chaos and be still.

The force of water on your soul

can bind itself to your Will.

I'll put you on the waves,

so you might reach the sky -

I'll give you endless stars

as the constellations swivel by.

Bring your wishes to my shore -

know your dreams, I'll help you find them.

By day, the sun, by night, the moon,

look upon my face for diamonds.

I walked to water's edge with heavy mind -

it seemed the only choice.

I walked to sit alone in silence -

by myself to withhold my voice.

The blue frothed white before my eyes,

and on my skin I felt the mist.

I claimed this time as only mine -

I calmed my heart, and I wished.

The moon pulled the body for me to see;

I heard the sound of tide on water's twist -

and having seen the dance performed

allowed me to only be and just exist.

3   **It Rained**

It rained across the saddest souls -

the bleakest and the most depressed.

It rained upon the happy folks -

the well loved and highest blessed.

The rain came down on those with nothing,

those hungry and impoverished.

It rained above the wealthy,

whose lives are rich and polished.

The plants and flowers felt the rain

and received it uncomplaining;

and it rained on structures and the houses,

which didn't know that it was raining.

     People on the Shore

I drive a road that claims for miles

a strip of sand and Huron stretching out.

I often see silhouettes in ones and twos

of people walking round and about.

I've seen them standing, posing, walking dogs,

and what looks like blankly staring.

And these pensive ones make me wonder -

I consider how their lives are faring.

I wonder if they're doing well,

or if they suffer in their lives.

I wonder if they come to feel

the thing that water best describes.

I wonder if they live here,

or if they come from another place.

What compels them to this shore,

what do they see on Huron's face?

5   **Looking at the Water**

I approached the sparkle of light upon the water.

I, a mortal with a finite body made of water,

whose soul is connected and attracted to the water,

find myself entranced while looking at the water.

6   Out of Chaos

Alone, along, all that great power -

bound by discourse and then made free.

Then light was light as light would be,

there to brood and shine above the sea -

came bursting forth the seed, the weed, and then the tree!

The angels looked and paused in awe -

they passed to watch and stopped to stare -

as one by one - from the water - we evolved.

7   **River**

Pressed upon the water's face,

were visions of my life to see -

and as the river pulled me forth,

I saw myself becoming me.

The water changed when I looked back,

moving forward, it was new.

I must be that living water,

and transformation is what I must do.

8   Fog

When spring is early and the buds are new,

the fog rolls in like a phantom in the air -

or like a goddess hiding soldiers

you wouldn't know were there.

Image of two seasons past -

the Halloween for which some yearn -

omen on blooms as they are birthing -

the death of Fall will return.

I hear water and hear sentiment -

I hear water and it seems to fit

whatever mood was brought too close,

whatever lingering thought was brought to it.

I hear a calling when I'm sad,

when I approach a lonesome shore,

to drown my sadness in the water,

for pain the water won't ignore.

I hear peace as pebbles roll beneath

transparent water in its shallow parts -

countless are the water pebbles,

and countless, too, peaceful hearts.

Water is like language,

more out there than I'll ever use.

Language is the sound and look of thought,

the expression of a muse.

So, then, thoughts are water, too -

clear only at the surface

then into darkness out of view.

We may walk or wade or dive into the deep.

We may stay in shallows or completely on the shore.

Thoughts need not be secrets we must keep,

but revelations waiting to be explored.

As with water, thoughts can be

something and somewhere to confide in -

a place where looking, mythic minds

will maybe see Poseidon.

11   Storm

There is movement in the sky

as the clouds appear and shift -

and a feeling down on Earth

as winds blow quick and swift.

Leaves break from twigs left behind

and tumble through the air,

and light on Earth gets dim a bit,

a smiling sky takes on a glare.

I make haste to get indoors,

to beat the rain before it starts -

I rush the yard to move the flowers,

like saving precious works of art.

Then from a window or the porch,

my skin moves when thunder sounds -

I wish for plenty bolts across the sky,

as Heaven sends its water to the ground.

12   Morning on a Small Lake

As mist rises on the inland lake,

lost in a forest as if plucked from lore,

the light falls pale upon the water,

and calm water barely nudges at the shore.

I smell life undisturbed -

undeveloped and unfatigued -

lily pads above the muck -

a heron peeking through the weeds.

I hear nature humming in the morning,

within the lake and on the land.

I stare as if in a dream of water,

where ripples form by a fish's kiss or my own hand.

13   Did I See a Mermaid?

I was a child who played in water,

whose imagination strayed.

The lake was deep beyond kicking feet,

where the light of day began to fade.

Water of my young mind's fancy,

in the deep, I saw colors glimmer.

Leviathan I'd think at first,

a mermaid if the colors shimmered.

14   Petrichor[1]

When drops of rain fall down on dirt,

a deep down scent erupts - deploys -

from the earth into my nostrils,

where my soul connects the sense to joy.

As the sight of light dancing in a rainbow,

as the touch of a breeze upon my skin,

as the sound of nighttime rain on rooftops,

I know petrichor like an old and faithful friend.

---

[1] Petrichor (noun): a distinctive, earthy, usually pleasant odor that is associated with rainfall especially when following a warm, dry period and that arises from a combination of volatile plant oils and geosmin released from the soil into the air (Merriam-Webster).

15   Shower

I took a shower when I was mad.

I washed my hair and washed my face.

When I dried off, I wasn't great,

but I didn't feel as bad.

I took a shower when I was stressed,

when I could not form words from thoughts.

Overwhelmed, the water beat me,

a therapy that can't be bought.

I took a shower so I could dwell -

my mood, by water, facilitated -

when I stepped out and dried myself,

I went forth to be creative.

I came upon a fountain in a dark and shady forest,

a perfect circle made of marble and hand-carved stone.

On the outer ring looped angels calming sea monsters

and other figures divine and human from a mythology unknown.

The inner ring on upper pedestal was charmed with prancing deer,

at their feet was molded flora found about the forest floor.

The highest tier held a giant vase wreathed in vines,

and from inside the pot is where water once gathered and outpoured.

But on that day, no water flowed from that great fountain,

the stone was dry, and grass and moss half covered it in green;

and all around were signs of movement lost to time long ago,

sunken foundations barely there, a broken heritage unseen.

I had come years too late to see the work as intended,

with water making beauty for what I could only guess was there.

I marveled at the fountain, thought of water on its surface,

and imagined a rippling basin, as I stood quietly and stared.

Part Two

Memories

We forget that water and life cycles are one.

25

Jacques Cousteau

17   Reed Lake

My parents left their lives by the city,

they didn't read Thoreau.

A new beginning was at hand

was all they had to know,

and then the family moved Up North

into the woods to live and grow.

Above Reed Lake in the Manistee,

still it's there on the land -

the home they made for their kids -

a chalet palace built by their hands;

and there my childhood forever rests,

may it be forever grand.

18   The Raft

There was a place I used to know,

I think of it every now and then -

a piece of childhood in the past

that I can never have again -

but my mind still summons what was mundane,

a memory to move my pen.

In early life, the raft let me know

what it means when something is serene -

placed on a lake smooth as glass,

a mirror for the surrounding scene -

the trees rising on the surrounding hills,

the house up top, peaking through the leafy green.

You were first to show me water's roar,

in Ludington with child's eyes;

and across your waves on another shore,

an ivory tower to make me wise.

But on that shore the time ran out,

I didn't know what to do.

I stayed and stumbled all about,

and despite resistance always knew -

I let myself give in to doubt -

home remained the other side of you.

I see myself upon your face,

an image of great worth.

For me you are a holy place,

you are profundity on Earth.

The sun is brilliant when you meet,

Hiawatha breathes on you.

I was not whole but went complete.

When I first left you, I was new.

21   **The Pigeon**

One midday, I went walking, unaccompanied, no friends or talking,

over the streets and sidewalks of Chicago's downtown space.

While I walked, nearly skipping - suddenly - there came a ripping,

as of a force roughly stripping, stripping the city of its grace.

I said, "It is nothing, nothing, nothing, stripping the city of its grace."

       And I still knew I loved that place.

Ah, distinctly I recall, it was at the start of Fall,

and beads of light danced on Lake Michigan's great face.

Oh how bad I wished to stay, but my heart had looked away,

gone was the golden day - the day of living well within that place.

I got what I had come for, and time had come to leave that place -

       to cross the water to find grace.

And the muted, muffled sound thundering all around

told me my imagined future had all but been erased.

Then I felt within my core a thought unfelt before,

a yearning that I swore would never pull me from that place.

The time had come to cross the water, for the city lost its grace.

       The time had come to leave that place.

Until then, the city's noise was something I enjoyed,

but in that moment it turned my outlets into utter waste.

There was the autos' endless rattle and the walkers' stifled babel,

the noise around me scrabbled what was good about that place,

and I craved the peace and silence of another place -

      across the water to find grace.

Then I saw the flirt and flutter of a flock of birds around the gutter,

a group unmoved by human footsteps that would not be displaced.

One gray bird with feathered hues of violet, green, and blue -

my soul it saw and knew - stepped to confront me to my face -

saying, "It is time for you to leave this place,

      for the city lost its grace."

And the pigeons kept on pecking while the beggars kept on begging,

I stood a step above, but only labor that is easily replaced.

Those pigeons lost the need to fear us, and indeed to eat they need us;

they should have seed, fruit, and nuts, but they're eating garbage in that place.

The flock remained, but that one confronting pigeon vanished without a trace -

      across the water to find grace.

22   Lake Huron

You make me know that I small,

as I stand by you beneath the sky.

Yet you give me big ideas -

inspiration and this is why.

You are word and image all around,

stories, paintings, memories -

of leisure, commerce, and livelihood -

a symbol for all the lives you claimed.

And I think I know for sure

that you and I are quite the same -

sometimes calm with quiet peace,

sometimes thrashing around untamed.

About the Author

Vincent Moyet is a poet, diarist, and creative nonfiction writer. He lives and writes in a small town on Lake Huron.

Other Titles by Vincent Moyet

A Restaurant Story

Rhyming Michigan: Poems About the Great Lakes State

Images from 1968 & 1969: The Vietnam War

Forthcoming from Vincent Moyet

Rhyming Michigan: The Haunted Places

Rhyming Michigan: All Four Seasons

The Hoffas' Vinyls